ANGEL'S VIEW OF CALVARY

POETRY FOR THE SOUL

ERIC LAWRENCE FRAZIER MBA

THE POWER IS NOW MEDIA, INC.
RADIO | TV | MAGAZINE | SEMINARS

CONTENTS

ANGEL'S VIEW OF CALVARY

Poetry for the Soul

By

Eric Lawrence Frazier, MBA

***

Thank you for taking the time to order and support my very first poetry collection. I just have one more request. If you could head over to Amazon and leave a 5-star review.

Reviews are the lifeline for any author and this will help other readers find and enjoy my book.

Best,

Eric L. Frazier

SCAN ME

POETRY COLLECTION BY ERIC LAWRENCE FRAZIER, MBA

ERIC LAWRENCE FRAZIER, MBA POETRY BOOKS

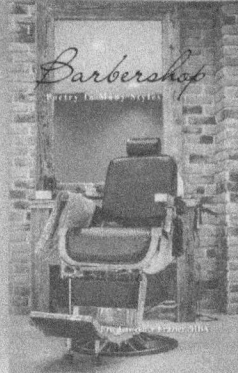

COPYRIGHT

ANGEL'S VIEW OF CALVARY
Poetry For The Soul

Copyright © 2025
The Power Is Now Media
Volume 3

www.ThePowerIsNow.com
@ThePowerisnow

ISBN-13: 978-1-949722-05-5 (ebook)
ISBN-13: 978-1-949722-02-4 (hardcover)

ACKNOWLEDGEMENT

First, I would like to thank God and the inspiration that He provides me to write. I love the Love of God and I am humbled to be saved by his grace and mercy. This book is dedicated to all who know Him and to those who are still searching. May you find Him. I want to thank my beautiful wife Ruby of 39 years. I love you more than words can say. You have been my rock and my greatest cheerleader from the day we first met. There is not a day that goes by that I am not grateful for all you have done and continue to do for our family and me. I can't imagine life without you. Thank you to my for wonderful daughters Jessica, Briana, Erica and Raela. Each one of you holds a special place in my heart. You are powerful, beautiful and highly intelligent women who are doing great things in life. I am very proud of all of you. To my grandchildren Carrah, Chloe and Cameron I love you very much and cannot wait to see the impact you have on the world. To Virgil and Jordan, you are men of God and of valor. I am thankful for the love you have for Briana and Raela and the life you are making together. I love you both and I am proud to be your father-in-law and for the blessing you are to my family. You all inspire me by the very different lives you're living and great things you are accomplishing. I am very proud to be the Patriarch of the family and I love you all very much.

Thank you, Kim Collier, Director of The Power Is Now Publishing. Your daily support, reminders, and expertise in publishing this book have been extremely valuable. I started with a vision and now we are publishing several books. Thank you for staying on me and working with me through the entire process. This book would not have happened without you. Thank you Goldy Ponce, Graphic designer and leader of The Power Is Now Graphic Design team, your amazing eye for design coupled with your ability to implement exactly what I need has resulted in an amazing cover that captures the true essence of this book. To Val Salomaki and Sheila Gilmore, both leaders of our Technology and Marketing team, you are awesome! It is because of your daily support, great work and professionalism that this book and others will receive the attention they deserve. I appreciate your work very much.

To those of you who are reading this book right now, thank you for taking a chance on me, and the time out of your busy life, to read my poetry. I hope you enjoy the book and share it with others.

DEDICATION

I dedicate this book of poetry to my father, Eddie Lawrence Frazier, who is living in heaven and enjoying the fruit of his faith. Without his influence and spiritual leadership, I would not have been able to write a book about the angel's view of Calvary. My father led me to Christ and provided the foundation for my understanding of God and my eternal destiny. He influenced me to go into preaching at a very young age and to serve in the ministry. Because of his faith, and his planting of the seed of faith in my heart, I dedicate this book to him.

PREFACE

"Angel's View of Calvary" is a special poem because it is the result of an otherworldly experience. Some of my best poetry is written when I am transported to a different realm and begin to write what I see. For "Angel's View of Calvary," I wrote what I saw in my mind and what I could visualize in Scripture.

The scene of Calvary as described in Scripture captures my imagination every time I read about it. But, imagine being an angel in Heaven, and witnessing Calvary from the beginning to the end. The arrest, beatings, suffering, and ultimately the crucifixion of our Lord and Savior Jesus Christ. Imagine being one of His Angels in heaven, and witnessing everything happening in real time, and wanting to do something about it.

Especially the Angels who were mighty men of God created to carry out his work on earth. Can you imagine them standing on the edge of heaven, watching the mocking, cruelty, and the suffering that Jesus was experiencing? The scriptures tell us about how the disciples responded in fear, the cruelty of the soldiers and the indifference of the people, but there is not one written word about what was happening with the host and inhabitants of heaven.

These thoughts formed the foundation of the poem "Angel's View of Calvary." Jesus Christ has risen from the grave and because He lives we can embrace the present and face tomorrow.

~Eric Lawrence Frazier, Poet

PRAISE

Father, the scriptures say you inhabit the praise of your people.

Let my heart be a place of habitation for you, Lord,

Let my tongue be the revealer of truth, Lord,

Let my tongue be the instrument of praise, Lord,

Let my tongue be the source of comfort from your word, Lord,

Let my tongue be the ambassador of peace, Lord,

Let my tongue be subject to your spirit, Lord,

Let my tongue proclaim the need for salvation to a dying world, Lord,

Let my tongue stop the mouths of the antichrists, Lord,

Let my tongue rally congregations to great works, Lord,

Let my tongue bring glory to you in everything, Lord,

Let my tongue bring forth joy in the midst of suffering, Lord,

Let my tongue bring forth peace in the midst of confusion, Lord,

Let my tongue bring forth love in the midst of hate, Lord,

Let my tongue bring forth truth in the midst of lies, Lord,

Let my tongue bring glory to you in everything, Lord,

Let my tongue be filled with prayers of thanksgiving, Lord.

Like the sweet-smelling savor of the sacrifices of old that went up before you Lord.

Now the joyful sounds of praise and spiritual sacrifices of prayers go before you, Lord.

Inhabit my heart, Lord, and fill my tongue with Praise.

THE LOVE OF GOD

The love of God is seen in the smiling face of a wife adoring her husband.

It is heard in the sounds of laughter of children playing with

their father,

It is felt on a cold Sunday morning in the warm embrace of a

mother,

It is seen in the sweet communion of friends, sisters and

brothers.

The love of God is interwoven in every aspect of life

Like the transparent cords that hold up a puppet

It is the means by which we interact and do what is right.

Invisible to the eye but clearly seen in our lives,

We should never be surprised

When we see the love of God carried out in disguise.

It is truly God's love disguised in the flesh of humanity

That helps us keep our sanity.

When you see so much violence and tragedy

You can't help but trust God, for He is the remedy.

Jesus said He would never leave us nor forsake us,

We can rejoice because God has not left us.

We see, hear and feel him because he has placed his law of

love in us.

It is witnessed in our actions, conversations, benevolence

and compassion,

It causes us to establish loving relationships and to live a life

full of passion.

I love the love of God and how he covers us,

He holds us up and promises a love surplus.

YOU ARE MORE THAN ENOUGH

"And God said, Let us make man in our image, after our likeness: and let them have dominion over the fish of the sea, and over the fowl of the air, and over the cattle, and over all the earth, and over every creeping thing that creepeth upon the earth. So God created man in his own image, in the image of God created he him; male and female created he them. And God blessed them, and God said unto them, Be fruitful, and multiply, and replenish the earth, and subdue it: and have dominion over the fish of the sea, and over the fowl of the air, and over every living thing that moveth upon the earth."

Genesis 1:26-28 KJV

One minute you are single.

The next you are married.

One minute you are a husband or wife.

The next minute you are a father or mother.

One minute you are a couple.

The next minute you are divorced or perhaps a widow.

One minute you are an employee.

The next minute you are unemployed.

One minute you are a homeowner.

The next minute you are a renter.

One minute you live in your house.

The next minute you live in a shelter.

One minute you have your health.

The next minute you are terminally ill.

Why do people go crazy and feel out of control?

Because this world is crazy and out of control.

The world is not where you find your identity.

Who you are cannot be seen in material externalities.

Nor does it exist in your ever-changing status in life.

Who you are cannot be found in a daily fight

Nor in your tenuous and volatile relationships

You have with your husband or wife.

Who you are does not rest in your appearance.

The style of your hair or the color of your eyes,

The length of your legs or thickness of your eyebrows,

Your height, weight, skin color or complexion,

Nor your education or facial expressions.

None of this is who you are, but it is what you do.

It all plays a role in how we view ourselves.

And how we behave and feel and respond to others.

Even when we have our coffee or wine or smoke or drug.

When we put on new clothes,

Shoes or cut our hair and make ourselves up.

We can practically float on air.

We don't have a problem or a single care,

In the world.

Just a change in clothes, a shot of this, a puff of that,

And a sip of something strong and we have

Forgotten about our problems -even our identity is gone,

But not for long.

A new cut, a new look, and an altered state of mind.

You are not fine. After the drugs, and wine and a little time

The novelty of it all wears off,

And once again you have lost your mind.

Back to that poor self-image,

Born out of your Ever-changing status,

In the world from which your identity has been formed.

You think you are going crazy because you are,

You now know that this is the norm,

And that you don't know who you are.

You are more than what you think you could ever be,

because you are more than your mind.

This understanding can only come with maturity

That takes time.

You are more than what you think because you are more than mind.

Your mind can be controlled and can control you

To live for the future.

Full of fears of failure or hope for success and for the past,

That is full of pain and regrets that seem to last.

Never allowing you to live in the present,

Where love, peace and life, as it is, can be enjoyed.

The present is where God is and you are enough to God.

You are not the sum of your past nor will you become more

In the future. You are who you are now.

It's time to meet the real you.

So where do you find you? You are here,

You are now, You are present and You are alive.

. . .

Alive with God who is omnipresent. God is not subject to

Time, space or place. God just is and created you to be in His

Image and more than what you think or could ever imagine

And more than enough now.

Believe it to be so because you can.

Just like you believe in everything else you do,

To find out who you really are.

Just be still, be present and be like your Imagine.

You can believe that you are perfect and wonderfully made.

You can believe that you are beautiful and valued.

You can believe that you are loved and adored.

You can believe that God rejoices over you,

You can believe you are His and His alone.

You can believe that you are the result of

His Love and sacrifice

You can believe that your life is not your own,

It was created in the Image of God so be THAT image.

And Be Great. Be audacious. Be perfect. Be wonderful

Be Beautiful. Be Handsome. Be Joyful. Be Creative.

Be Happy. Be Kind. Be Grateful.

Be Forgiving. Be Valued. Be loved.

Be Adored. Be celebrated. Be present and Be Enough.

Be You.

Because God made you,

And you are enough.

Right NOW!

BLESS YOU

*B*less you, as you go on your way,

I pray my thoughts will brighten your day.

I hope in your journey you'll always remember,

The fellowship we treasure year after year with great pleasure.

Leaving with no regrets, no sorrows, no tears,

As you leap out in faith, confronting your fears.

Begin a fresh new start,

Put God in your plan to capture

The dreams and desires of your heart.

I will miss you, I must admit,

But to my sad emotions I will not submit.

Follow your dreams and keep God in your plan,

And all the things He promises will stand.

MARRIAGE

I love the idea of marriage,

    The intense care and love that exists in marriage,

The children that come as a result of marriage,

The families that are bound together forever in marriage,

The maturity that couples develop in marriage.

I love the traditions that exist in marriage,

The lives that are built together in marriage,

The stuff that is accumulated in marriage,

The history that is created in marriage,

The great things that are achieved because of marriage.

I love the love in marriage,

The love that is established in marriage,

The love that grows in marriage,

The love-making that gets better in marriage,

The love that strengthens each other's weaknesses in marriage.

I love that God is the foundation of marriage,

The authority God has in the marriage,

the prayers that go up to God for marriage,

The unity and spirituality that God brings in marriage,

The forgiveness that God requires in marriage,

The blessings that God has granted in marriage.

Marriage has blest me to see

The power and the love of God working in me.

It is incredible to see how we have become three,

And then three became four

And we needed another bedroom door.

And then four became five

and I thought I had lost my mind.

And then five became six

and she said it was time to quit.

So off I went to stop the events

Because I couldn't afford rent,

Just to feed these children,

Any money I earned was already spent.

I look at life now and all I can do is smile.

I know God was right, even though it took a while

To watch them grow up and live life with style.

What would I be if I were not married to Ruby,

Is a question hard to consider completely.

Having my life connected to my wife has made

Marriage and family complete my identity.

All I know is that one flesh we have become.

Husband and wife forever, she is second to none.

In spite of my weaknesses, her love for me has never gone.

She finds ways to support me regardless of what I have done.

I thank God that there is a Ruby that loves me,

Because deep down I know that marrying her,

Undoubtedly saved me.

GOOD GROUND

*S*tones, thorns and good ground

    Are all homes where the seed of faith is sown?

Stony, thorny and good ground

Are the hearts that must be broken or plowed

For seeds to be found?

Lord, when I heard the Gospel it shook me to my bone

I knew I wanted God to be my father and Heaven my future home.

When I heard the Gospel it was like a heavy weight being lifted off of me

And blinders taken off my eyes so that I could see,

My heart of stone was crushed into pieces and I believed

In the Savior Jesus.

. . .

It was like a plow that went straight through me,

Pulling all the weeds away so that I could see,

It was like the rain that would not stop falling

And flooded my heart and gave me a new calling.

I thank you, Father, for drawing me

And helping me to see my need for thee,

I was lost, but have been found,

Because my faith in your Son is pure and sound.

Thank you for breaking my heart and making me good ground.

MY HEART CRIED TODAY

y heart cried today,

Because of the chaos and dismay that the world is going through.

My heart cried today,

For the victims' families that lost their loved ones.

My heart cried today,

As I heard the radio stations flooded with calls offering condolences.

My heart cried today,

Because today is the day to remember and never forget.

My heart cried today,

Because we as a nation were not prepared for such an attack.

My heart cried today,

Because of the lack of peace and fear that we have in the world today.

My heart rejoiced today,

Because we have decided to stay strong.

My heart rejoiced today,

Because as believers we have nothing to worry about. Our future is secure because He keeps us always in the present.

My heart rejoiced today,

Because adversity makes us stronger individually and collectively.

My heart rejoiced today,

Because I am here fighting this battle with you.

MY STRENGTH

*H*ow paradoxical my strength is to me,

For in my weakness I am as strong as I can be.

Contrary to what others might see,

God is my strength and only He.

He takes care of all my endless wants and needs,

All I have to do is follow his lead.

Occasionally I forget that he is my strength indeed,

And become his rival in meeting my needs.

In my weakness God has accessibility,

To show that man's extremity is his opportunity.

When I am weak, then I am strong,

And can do battle with the enemy who rages on,

Seeking to kill me and to tear away my faith,

God is always on time and has never been late.

What can my little old strength do anyway?

To mention it is almost senseless to say.

Can I create the air I breathe?

Or make the earth bear fruit on trees?

Can I stop the wind from blowing?

Or the floods from destroying?

Can I keep my heart beating throughout eternity?

Or on my own awakened from death's slumber to face reality?

I can do all things through Christ who strengthens me,

He is my rock in weakness,

And He will always be.

I LOVE THE LOVE OF GOD

The God of Love is the best part of me,

He covers my weakness and protects me,

I am so blessed that He abides in me.

He is faithful when I am unfaithful,

He is truthful when I am untruthful,

He is loving when I am unloving,

He is caring when I am uncaring,

He is giving when I am not giving.

His Love empowers me,

And challenges me to be,

The Godly man that He would have me be.

. . .

Faithful because He is faithful,

Truthful because is He truthful,

Loving because He is loving,

Caring because He is caring,

Giving because He is giving.

The Love of God lives through me

So that He can be seen through me.

To give him all the credit,

Because out of the abundance of His grace

He has chosen me.

BLESSED

I am so blessed – I do not know where to begin,

  So I think the place I'll start is with my sins,

I am so glad that at a young age I was born again.

Jesus has been a part of my life for years,

And has cleansed me from all my sins,

I am so blessed that I can depend on Him

Knowing that He will be there for me through thick and thin.

He alone, not me, has my soul to win,

No longer will I live in fear of the end,

Or of the judgment coming for those who have rejected Him.

I look forward to the day that I win,

I look forward to a new home and a new body

All because Jesus died for my sins.

I am so blessed – I do not know where to begin,

With thanksgiving to God for His love,

And to Jesus for being my greatest friend.

WHEN I READ MY BIBLE

The Spirit of Truth has set me free.

When I sit down and read my Bible, I say to the Spirit,

"Speak to me Spirit, and cut me in two again."

You do that better than anyone who is a truth teller.

You don't care about my feelings that day,

Or whether or not things have been going my way.

You just infuse it into my heart and go to work on me,

Bringing to light thoughts unacceptable to thee,

Actions past, present and future that are reprehensible,

Your Word cuts me to the marrow of my bone,

It pierces my heart and makes me moan.

It causes me to repent for the moment,

And then I go back,

To the same old sins again,

Those evil thoughts flowing again,

Actions reprehensible again,

And so, I need a whooping.

Like a rebellious child who will not listen,

Who needs to go to the whipping tree and find his own switch,

And get corrected old-country style,

When not sparing the rod was saving the child.

When I sit down and read my Bible I say to the Spirit,

"Spirit, help me, take me, force me and walk with me,

Make me be the person I have been called to be."

With my voice raised to shouting, I exclaim,

I can't help me,

I need Jesus to save me from myself.

Myself, that's the enemy I see.

Not the devil – defeated enemies are no threat to me,

I don't need the whipping tree,

Because Jesus took a whipping for me.

But why can't I live perfectly?

By the grace He has provided for me,

Jesus died willingly,

Rose from the grave for me,

Gave a life of eternity,

What other motivation do I need to live for Him?

To make my life a model for Him,

Strive to get to know Him,

So that I can reflect Him

In my life.

But here I go again,

Back to the same old sins again,

Those evil thoughts flowing again,

Actions reprehensible again,

And so, I need a whooping.

Grace came, but nothing has changed.

I still see the sin in me,

Totally unable to change on my own,

I need the power of the Son.

But I have Him already?

Okay – so what's the deal with me?

The reality is that He is with me,

His righteousness has clothed me,

Covered my sins completely

Set me free and gave me liberty.

So I serve him freely,

In spite of the sin I see in me,

And the whoopin's that come frequently,

Because I serve the law of sin,

With the flesh He gave me,

And I serve the law of God.

With the mind He is renewing in me.

It's His thing, not mine.

It's His power, not mine.

I had nothing to do with it.

He is just living in sinful me.

My Brother is in me. Wow!

My Brother! My Elder Brother! My Man! My God!

My High Priest and Chief Bishop of my soul. Wow!

Look who You are to me!

O sin, where is thy power?

O death, where is thy sting?

O grave, where is thy victory?

O Lucifer, son of light, where is thy authority?

It's not over me!

Yet here I go again,

Back to the same old sins again,

Those evil thoughts flowing again,

Actions reprehensible again,

And so, I need a whoopin because I know better.

Some people are just hardheaded.

So don't trip on us,

Just line up behind us,

Support us, and get your free on.

Because we are free!

In spite of the sin you see.

Thank God that my God's love for me,

Is not because of the goodness in me,

Or because of your judgments of me.

I am free!

DISCIPLESHIP

Have you tried to pay the cost of discipleship?

But always come up short?

Thinking that the cost was perfection,

Are you constantly out of sorts?

One day I heard something about Jesus,

Who I thought I knew before,

That when He came and died on the cross,

My sins, and yours, were completely paid for.

Jesus came to die for me,

He is my perfection, not me, you see,

He is the one whom Isaiah prophesies,

Would pay the penalty of death for me.

. . .

He died to pay my debt of sin,

That so easily beset me, I can never win.

What a marvelous gift I have received.

Jesus laid his life down for me.

After having my sin all wiped away,

Being redeemed and saved by His grace,

I thank God for putting my faith in Him

And that He is running my race.

Hallelujah! I have been born again!

No more worries about my debt of sin,

Jesus Christ took it all in,

And rose victorious over death, the grave and sin.

Now I'm just living life with Jesus, my only friend

And waiting for Him to come again,

The Victory to Win!

THE GOSPEL

The Gospel is my reality,

Without it Christ's life would be a fallacy,

And in this life there would be no hope for me,

To live with God in eternity.

So I believe the Gospel with all my heart you see,

It's not just Good News but the Best News for me.

To know that Jesus died for me,

Empowers me to be all that I can be:

A stalwart apologist for Christianity.

He set me free from sin and death you see,

Gave me a new life and by faithI am set free

My new body, my new home

And my eternity.

THE ANGEL'S VIEW OF CALVARY

We were flying in and out of the heavens,

Looking after the universe,

And taking care of the Creator's children as usual,

When I saw what was happening to the Son of God.

He had taken upon himself the sins of the world

And fulfilled all that the prophets had proclaimed

And what He upon earth had heralded.

And we were stunned,

Because we didn't really imagine that day would come.

His soul was overwhelmed with sorrow to the point of absent breath.

For He foreknew the magnitude of His suffering and death.

And when we heard His cry in Gethsemane,

"My Father, if it is possible,

May this cup be taken from me."

We were certain that His death would not be a reality.

But the Father's will was His reality and so it was done.

It was done.

He left heaven and emptied himself of His glory.

It was done.

He put on human flesh and became a servant.

It was done.

He humbled himself and submitted to a torturous death.

It was done.

Our Lord! Was on his way to a rich man's tomb.

We are all so in awe of our God and His Son,

He is an ever-present reality before us on his throne.

Any movement or declaration He would make

Would signal the angelic host of Heaven to come.

Our home is a place of unspeakable beauty,

And majesty full of light continuously,

It is the home of your majesty, The Most High God.

We cannot describe it completely,

In words that you can understand,

For we speak in a language that is otherworldly,

And your mind cannot comprehend.

We speak of heaven's beauty among ourselves,

In angelic prose, divine quatrains and limericks,

That leap from our hearts that God composed.

We are instruments of praise,

Created for His purpose,

To carry out his every will and command,

And oversee his human test.

The Most High God is magnificent.

His beauty is incomprehensible.

The love that emanates from His light,

Conjures up a sea of unimaginable,

Joyful weeping and happiness.

When you come to see and know the One God, you are truly blessed.

Everyone will come to know

The eternal love and grace our God bestows

and to behold His presence like the brightness of an eternal day.

Hair like wool, skin like bronze and feet like clay.

His likeness resembles that of jasper and carnelian

Engulfed in a warm, soft light.

His presence penetrates your soul and evokes deep within you

A love and adoration of Him,

That overwhelms you.

A halo, resembling an emerald, encircles His throne.

It symbolizes His omniscience, omnipotence and omnipresence.

For He is Jehovah God and,

Beside Him there is no one.

I marveled and thousands and thousands,

And ten thousand upon ten thousand angels,

Marveled with me as we witnessed the demise of the Son.

God's earthly children thought they were undone

But this was necessary so that they could be reborn.

I marveled and thousands and thousands

And ten thousand upon ten thousand angels marveled with me

As we witness Jehovah's great act of love, grace and mercy.

His immaculate conception and human incarnation,

His suffering and degradation, his passions and expiation.

All the host of Heaven wailed at His suffering and man's evil deed.

So moved by what we saw, we fell prostrate before Jehovah,

And asked, "How could this be?"

Before he answered, we heard the Son cry,

"Eli, Eli, lama sabachthani!"

"My God, my God, why hast thou forsaken me?"

We jumped to the ready, our wings spanned ten feet,

Swords drawn and stretched forth,

We shouted with such rage, that the heavens shook,

And the sun stood still and stopped its shining.

We flew to the very edge of the earth's atmosphere,

And waited like ravenous wild Lions who hadn't eaten for days.

We waited anxiously for Jehovah's command,

To descend and rescue the Son of Man.

We waited nervously for His word,

And the mighty thunderbolts of heaven,

To destroy his enemies and purge the leaven.

But Jehovah held his peace and our sword.

Sin had completed its work,

And Death was allowed to have the last word.

God said that He must give up life,

That the world might have eternal life.

We marveled at His incredible act of love and sacrifice.

Our voices and the voices of many angels,

Numbering thousands upon thousands,

And ten thousand times ten thousand,

Filled the eternal dwellings of heaven

With sounds of praise and adoration,

And wailing and moaning for God's Son.

For we had witnessed something that heretofore was inconceivable:

The death of God.

Then the throne of God erupted,

With flashes of lighting,

And peals of thunder.

Surrounding the throne,

Were twenty-four other thrones.

Seated on them,

Were twenty-four elders.

They were dressed in white,

And had crowns of gold up on their heads.

Before the throne there was what appeared to be a sea of glass.

In the center, around the throne, were four living creatures.

They were covered with eyes in front and in back.

The first living creature was like a lion,

The second was like an ox,

The third had a face like a man,

The fourth was like a flying eagle.

Each of the four living creatures had six wings

And was covered with eyes all around, even under his wings.

Day and night they never ceased to say:

"Holy, holy, holy is the Lord God Almighty,

Who was, and is, and is to come."

The twenty-four elders fell down before His throne

And laid their crowns before the throne, saying:

"You are worthy, our Lord and God,

To receive glory and honor and power

For you created all things, and by your will,

They were created and have their being."

Then one of the elders said to the throng of angels

Hovering above the throne,

"Do not weep! The Lion of the tribe of Judah,

The Root of David, the Son of Man has triumphed."

Then we saw Him on earth -

The Lamb of God, resurrected,

Looking as if it had been slain,

Having suffered the pain,

Of being born into death.

Nail prints in his hands and feet,

A stab wound in His side, but He could speak.

He proclaimed his power in Heaven and Earth.

He summoned us and we came:

Thousands and thousands and ,

Ten thousand upon ten thousand angels with me,

Invisible to those on earth to see.

We picked Him up and ascended together to Heaven's throne room

And stood with him on the right hand of Jehovah

Standing in the center of the throne

Encircled by the four living creatures and the elders.

He took the scroll from the right hand,

Of Him Who sat on the throne.

And when He had taken it, the four living creatures,

and the twenty-four elders fell down before the Lamb.

Each one had a harp, and they were Holding golden bowls full of incense,

Which are the prayers of the saints.

And they sang a new song:

"You are worthy to take the scroll,

And to open its seals,

Because you were slain,

And with your blood,

You purchased men for God,

From every tribe and language,

And people and nation."

In a loud voice we his messengers, angels,

Numbering thousands upon thousands,

And ten thousand times ten thousand,

Encircling the throne sang:

"Worthy is the Lamb, who was slain,

To receive power and wealth and wisdom,

And strength and honor and glory and praise!"

Then I heard every creature in heaven and on earth,

And under the earth and on the sea,

And all that is in them, singing:

"To him who sits on the throne and to the Lamb,

Be praise and honor and glory and power, for ever and ever!"

The four living creatures said, "Amen",

The twenty-four elders said "Amen",

All the angels in Heaven said "Amen",

And the entire host of Heaven fell down and worshiped.

And still do to this very moment in time.

Just one angel's view of Calvary from here.

GOD'S MAKEOVER

We live in depression,

Because we are under the impression,

Of assigned identities that come in never-ending successions,

Born out of life-changing circumstances,

Manifesting themselves as our identity and our soliloquy

About who we are to be or not to be. That is the question.

Are we our circumstances and situations?

Mind created illusions and imaginations?

Are we parading our false Identities and

Giving them life instead of paying them never mind.

Accepting an Identity filled with pain and hopelessness,

Anesthetize with alcohol and drugs.

We are confused and lost.

We cannot face this crisis we have created ourselves,

With the identities, we have accepted from the world,

Or have heard so often about ourselves,

That we now believe and accept them as real.

They reside in our minds,

Not eternal but temporary finds.

Fleeting and constantly changing our minds

Offering something different every time.

The kind of life that God is offering,

Cannot be purchased and does not exist

In the external and circumstantial situations of life.

That is not life but the abyss.

The kind of identity that God is offering,

Cannot be developed through,

Hard work and determination.

The kind of identity that God is offering,

Cannot be achieved by joining clubs,

And various organizations.

The kind of identity that God is offering,

Cannot be found in a pill,

or bottle, or wilding behavior

The kind of identity that God is offering,

Is by way of spiritual Adoption,

Into God's family by faith,

In Jesus Christ His only option.

Your faith is the means by which the Word,

Brings about spiritual regeneration

Faith in the incarnation

Places you into God's familial congregation,

Welcome to the family and your new Identity by Faith.

There is no mountain to climb or ocean to swim.

There is no work to do. There are no tests to take.

You do not need to get dressed up or dressed down.

You don't have to change your hair, the color of your skin or eyes.

You can be Black, White, Asian, Middle Eastern, Native American, or unsure about your ancestry, all heritage or genealogy.

You don't have to have a job or even have an education.

You don't have to be married or unmarried.

You don't have to be heterosexual, bisexual, gender neutral, transgender or gay. Just come as you are without one plea.

Just be present.

Because you're more than the external form you see in the mirror.

He loves you just as you are.

Even though you cannot see who you really are,

You just know you are somebody more than what you see

And that you are from a source of intelligence, far greater than your mind.

You are a living soul, a spiritual being.

You have existed in space and time

Far beyond your chronological age.

God knew you before and in the womb.

There is You that exists in material form from the dust of ground and is limited by time and space.

And there is You created in the image of God whose characteristics you cannot see but know, because you are created in his image.

He is God, He is omnipresent, omniscient and Omnipotent.

Not bounded by flesh but unbound by Spirit. You are created in the image of God.

. . .

Your Intelligence is far beyond what you have learned, what you see, what you feel, and what you do or are capable of doing.

You are able to observe the very thoughts that your mind produces.

You are able to transcend your present form and see yourself from above or below or from the right or left and observe.

You do not need a mirror because you are spirit and your true self operates in a space that is present, the source of all intelligence that transcends all that you can see, or hear and your mind can comprehend.

It is the true intelligence that enables you to judge yourself and to criticize your thoughts and to ask where is this coming from or why am I doing this? These criticisms are coming from all the inputs from the world and your circumstances that reside in your mind.

But remember you are not your mind. Your mind is what you do and you must renew your mind all the time.

Your identity is not your mind. Your identity is Christ.

Now as a member of God's family,

Your identity is based on your relationship with God

As your Father and Christ as your Elder Brother.

You have eternal life, because You are eternal life.

It is your birthright as a child of Abraham through faith,

And God's unconditional love and forgiveness

That you have until He comes again.

Amen!

JESUS SAVED ME

When I looked up from my appointment with destiny

I saw the hand of Jesus reach out to me;

By faith, I grabbed ahold of His hand and He saved me

From myself and everything else around me.

I was covered by sin and iniquity;

Bloodstained hands from the enmity

That raged within me.

Striking out at everybody who I thought was against me;

I even fought against my own family

And against those who loved me,

Unable to love anybody, not even me.

I then began to see that Jesus died for me.

Oh how he demonstrated his love for me,

When no one else would die for me!

God the Father gave Him up for me.

He stretched forth His mighty hand and lifted me

Out of the muddy grave that was my destiny.

To die in a state of misery

Because I could not see the peace, joy and love that be

In Jesus who has made life so easily

To be set free and so I'm free.

From the evil within me;

To love the brothers and sisters I see;

Living in the streets with me;

Who are not willing to die for me

Like Jesus did for me.

Christ's death rocked the world and me;

His blood ran down Calvary;

Cleansed me of iniquity;

I cannot believe that all I have to do

Is believe in the Most High God.

How precious I must be

For God to show so much mercy to me!

THE YOKE OF SATAN, THE YOKE OF CHRIST

Matthew 11:28-30 NN
Come to me, all you who are weary and burdened, and I will give you rest. Take my yoke upon you and learn from me, for I am gentle and humble in heart, and you will find rest for your souls. For my yoke is easy and my burden is light.

The difference between the yoke of Satan and the yoke of Christ

Is that one requires living a burdened and weary life,

Living with fear because their life isn't right.

The other is at rest in their soul and at peace with their life

Totally secure about their relationship with Jesus Christ.

The yoke of Satan is full of despair,

These are the people who put on spiritual airs

But in reality they can hardly bear

The burden of their own unrighteousness,

Which is the yoke they wear.

Always depressed, living life insecure,

worried that the return of Christ is near.

Looking like the frozen eyes of fear,

When headlights happen upon a deer.

Religious to a cultic extreme

Always talking about sin and staying clean

Every other sentence is "Thank you, Jesus!" and

"Praise His name"

Even at sports games they will invoke his name

As if Jesus helped them win the game.

All of it is an act to cover the pain

That comes with not feeling eternally secure

By the cleansing blood of the Lamb who was slain.

The yoke of Satan will have you constantly on your knee

In prayer for the sin in your life that be

Or for anybody who has fallen into calamity

They pray to God, asking that their sins

Might be forgiven by thee.

They confess their sins in the morning and at night.

In every prayer they hope to be right

And at the end of their life

They find themselves before the prince of light.

They pray that they have done everything right:

Never missed a Sunday night,

Always paid tithes and gave whatever was right,

Never with a sister or brother did they fight,

Helped feed the hungry and gave the homeless a place for the night,

Never divorced, stayed married to one wife,

Raised beautiful children that were taught to live right,

Lord, he cries, I worked so hard to do right and be right

That I might be accepted into your kingdom of light.

Please tell me the destiny of my plight .

Having worked for you day and night

I have been worried oh so long,

That you might determine I was wrong.

That I slipped up that day or night,

Or got in a situation that wasn't right,

And didn't ask for forgiveness or make a confession

At churchWednesday night. Had not learned my lesson.

Please, Lord Jesus, let me into Heaven,

There shouldn't be too much sin that I've been in.

I think I've earned the right because I have not sinned

As much as other brothers and sisters and some of my friends.

I have been striving long and hard to live the Christian life –

Tired and weary from carrying this burden of "doing right".

I want to know that I am saved, that I am really accepted in your sight.

This yoke of yours that I wear has given me strife

I'm tired of it! Give me eternal life!

What's that, Father? Jesus gave up His life that I might have life?

You mean all this time, it has not been my life that has given me might?

You're not counting all the things that I did right?

Or counting all the things left undone, to this night?

Or counting all the evil that I did and said in Your sight?

What's that, Father? My life wasn't capable of right,

So you gave me Christ who gave up His life?

Because I wasn't right and have never been right.

Father forgive me!

I didn't know that I could do no right,

But only be made right for eternal life

by having faith in Jesus Christ.

I thought I was earning my way to Heaven in this life.

When all this time, I'd been right in your sight

Because of the fact that I have been born again

By faith in Jesus Christ!

Father, I have been deceived in thinking

That by my words and deeds I was right.

I didn't know it led me to living under the yoke of Satan

And not the yoke of Christ.

I rejoice in the fact that I have had on the yoke of eternal life

Ever since I came to faith in Jesus Christ,

I just didn't see him as the final sacrifice

For all the sins committed, for all whom I've caused strife.

Lord, I pray that men and women everywhere

Don't find themselves living a life of despair

Unsure if God has prepared a place for them in Heaven

And has them under His care.

If you have come to faith in Christ

Serve him out of love and gratitude for His life

Just like you do for your children, husband, wife

Instead of trying to merit eternal life.

Or living under a lie, the yoke of Satan

And not the yoke of Christ.

Thank you, Father, for the yoke of Christ

His yoke is easy and his burdens are light.

WALK BY FAITH, NOT BY SIGHT

2 Cor 5:7 KJV
"For we walk by faith, not by sight."

Walk by faith not by sight? Yeah, right!

If you could see the violence on my left and right,

The sadness that surrounds me day and night,

You would know why I walk by sight.

You think in my circumstances I can believe that people see the light

In this world of darkness, evil, and folks who ain't right?

Brother, I got to watch my back and pack light;

I got faith in my hommies who protect me and fight.

Who are you to tell me to walk by faith and not by sight,

When everything you got is slick and tight?

You're not worrying about where you're gonna sleep tonight,

Or if a gang-banger is going to take your life.

Any drive-bys happening on your street tonight?

You got money in the bank and living the good life;

Sitting in a house with kids, husband or a wife,

Driving a car instead of walking long hikes,

Eating three meals a day instead of trash-can delights.

You ain't living my life

Or going through the strife

That I deal with day and night.

Come to me, if you want to, with that faith and no sight,

And I'll hit you over the head; maybe I'll take your life!

What are you going to do then,

When I knock you out and take all your ends?

What's your faith going to do for you when

You can't pay rent or find your faithful Christian friends?

You got an angel who'll fly down and drop you some ends,

And restore your blindness so that you can walk by faith again?

Can your God get me a job?

Can He pay my rent or utilities or protect me from the mob?

Where is He for me? Can you show me?

Because I don't see

How this faith of yours can get me anything! It's up to me!

When you tell me to walk by faith and not by sight,

Just live in my shoes and you'll know why it doesn't sound right.

I don't know anybody trying to live that kind of life.

I'll take my chances walking by sight.

Will your faith give me peace in this life?

Will I have no more worries, pain, or strife?

It sounds good, but I know it's all hype!

~

Response

Hold up, my brother, you just don't see;

You can't blame your circumstances on Jesus—

maybe Washington, D.C.

He isn't the cause of the darkness and evil you see.

Don't kill your faith because of the apathy that be

Among His namesakes who walk by your circumstances, trying not to see

How you are crying out for help and that your faith in them is key

To help you believe that Jesus is the reality.

They say "be warmed and filled" without even a pause in their stride.

You end up looking at their backside and say Jesus must have lied,

Because all His followers do nothing but talk a lot of jive.

Don't let them rob you of your faith,

Just because so many of them are fake,

And the preachers you know are on the take,

Not really concerned about the difference they could make.

If you want someone to blame, then you got the wrong claim.

The Devil is his name; he is the prince of the air and driving this world insane,

Causing Christians to bring shame on Jesus' name,

Because their claim doesn't match their game.

Your mind is being raped of the faith because the Devil has a stake

In making sure you don't come to faith

In Jesus Christ, who kicked down hell's gate.

So brother, my brother, don't lose your mind.

You have no idea what kind of power that faith can have over time.

You think you have the answer to life's riddle or rhyme?

You actually think that you haven't been living by faith all this time?

Don't be a fool and deny the faith that is within thee,

Evidenced by life itself and God's creation that you see,

The testimonies of the Apostles that Jesus gave thee,

And the power of the Gospel that, if you believe, would save thee.

Walk by faith and you will see

That God is real and that He died on a tree.

But He rose on the third day to set you free

And grants you eternal life if by faith you can see

That He has given you peace, life, and hope for eternity.

God is real, and His Son's blood has sealed the deal.

He has covered you by His eternal will

And made sure that the law, sin, and death

Are no longer partners that can steal.

The joy and peace that the Spirit will seal,

If in your confession your faith is revealed.

So don't think that you have ever gotten through a single night

Because you have hommies with guns standing watch to daylight.

Don't you know that you can't control the Devil's night?

For if it wasn't for Jesus,

He could take you out tonight.

My advice to you is to walk by faith and not by sight,

For in Jesus Christ there is the abundant life.

(John 10:10 KJV)

"The thief cometh not, but for to steal, and to kill, and to destroy:

I am come that they might have life, and that they might have it more abundantly."

MY ROCK

Psalms 18:2

He is my Rock, I heard his call,

He's yours too, but to me it's personal.

My Rock, like no other Rock

Not a pebble or a stone

Of many pebbles or stones,

But my Rock.

My Rock in creation,

My Rock in redemption,

My Rock in regeneration,

My Rock where stability is

Instead of relationships that are constantly changing

My Rock when money comes and goes

To deal with life when full of trouble and woes.

My Rock where cities may fall

And ruins surrounds us all, he is my Rock.

In sickness, He is my Rock.

In uncertainty, He is my Rock.

In triumph, He is my Rock.

In defeat, He is my Rock.

In disappointment, he is my Rock.

In life, He is my Rock.

In death, He is my Rock.

He's mine, I belong to him.

He's yours too, but

To me it's personal.

GREAT AND PRECIOUS PROMISES

(2 Peter 1:4-8 MV)
The result of our faith is great and precious promises given by God.

*A*re we aware of this or do we think it is a façade?

Brother, we live by faith in the divine nature with God.

Right now we see how to escape the corruption of this world

caused by the evil desires that beguile us and rob

our hearts from the love of God.

So we add to our faith while on this spiritual road we trod

Things that will help us in fighting the evil desires that rob.

To faith we add goodness and to goodness knowledge.

To knowledge self-control and to self-control perseverance.

To perseverance godliness and to godliness brotherly kindness

and to brotherly kindness love.

Because God is love.

Embrace the divine nature and trust in God.

You will become the light of the world directing people to God

Or the salt of the earth preserving souls for God.

Don't be like salt that has lost it savor

And is cast out under the feet of men who trod,

Not when you have the precious promises

given by Almighty God.

DECEMBER NINETEENTH

That Month, that Day, that Hour, that moment in time
    When all of my hopes and dreams would be realized in a
few lines:

"Do you take this woman to be your wedded wife?

And do you solemnly promise,

Before God and these witnesses,

That you will love her, comfort her,

Honor and keep her in sickness and in health;

And that forsaking all others for her alone,

You will perform unto her all the duties

That a husband owes to his wife,

Until God, by death,

Shall separate you?"

To the preacher, who was my father, I exclaimed,

"I do!"

And from that time forward she took on my name:

Mrs. Ruby Frazier, she became.

Of all the people in the world, I thank God she chose me:

My love, my life, my lover, my wife,

For nineteen years we have been together in this life

I love you more with each day and each night

With all that is good and light.

These nineteen years have been the best of my life

I look forward to the twentieth year

Of blissful days and comforting nights.

THE WOLF IN SHEEP'S CLOTHING

Smooth, debonair, articulate, compassionate and spiritual.

Singer, preacher, teacher, counselor and reputable.

Father, husband, brother, businessman and leader

But most of all a preacher

And a wolf

In sheep's clothing, that is,

Taking advantage of the naïve,

The vulnerable and easy to deceive

Anyone, including me

I believed the lies, and couldn't see

Beyond the sheep's slick trickery.

He said it was his wife you see, that made life

A horrible reality of what marriage should be.

He had enough of her suspicions and accusations

Always calling him into question about his

Interactions with those of the female persuasion.

However, her suspicions proved to be legitimate

He had been lying about everything, never admitting it.

Fornication and adultery is his first and last name

Because sex outside of marriage is now his game.

One unsuspecting single mother he failed

As her minister and counselor because of his betrayal

Found herself under his spell.

Before she knew what happened and that he was married,

they were having sex in the backseat of his carriage.

She thought she was in love, and that she was his lady,

But the reality was that he played her – he had another lady, his wife.

This brother is shady but one day he will get his payday

When all his adulterous escapades drive him crazy.

It doesn't matter who you are or how you appear,

People will find out what's underneath the veneer.

Wolves in sheep's clothing are eventually exposed,

History's highway is scattered with stories untold,

Of how men and women sold their souls,

Because they would not kill the wolf inside,

Would not stop wearing the sheep's stylish hide.

TRIPPING OVER THE CHRISTIAN LIFE

~~~

(2 Cor 5:17 NW)
"Therefore, if anyone is in Christ, he is a new creation; the old has
gone, the new has come!"

Why are you tripping?

You can't live the Christian life!

Only Christ can, you lack the strength and might.

You live through His life

Because your life isn't right.

Be honest, haven't you messed up all your life –

And you continue to struggle to do what is right?

You can't remember the last time you slept through the night

And even lie in your prayers at night!

Don't think it's a secret that you are not right;

A whole bunch of people got you in their sight.

God only knows, what would be the testimony of your wife,

But yet you claim to be living the Christian life.

Brother, you are tripping over the Christian life!

Don't let me bring up what I heard last night -

That you have been messing around with somebody else's wife.

Or the fact that you are always getting in a fight

With some poor soul you think ain't right.

Saw you drunk the other night!

But if I say you can't live the Christian life

You'll fight me tooth and nail

That a Christian must have a sinless life.

To you, to teach anything else would be to deny Christ

And to license sin and evil in this life.

You really think you can't go to heaven with sin or not living right.

All the leaders of the church will say, "Amen! That's right!

But don't be tripping, poking your nose into our life."

Can't you see how they are tripping over the Christian life

And have cornered them into a hypocritical plight?

Because they know that they don't live a sinless life.

But try to be pious anyway and knowing we know that they ain't right.

. . .

Their own life is a testimony to everybody's plight

That ain't nobody living the Christian life!

This fact should bear witness to our position in Christ:

That our salvation isn't based on our struggle to do right;

But rests solely in our identity, and not a flawless life.

We have been made a new creation.

Not some type of Christ-like imitation.

If anything, we are the result of spiritual regeneration.

We have been re-created to possess eternal life.

That is the closest we can be to an imitation of Christ.

There are no imitations even if you think you live a perfect life.

Therefore, the life I live is Christ living in me.

I cannot live the Christian life without him

It is an impossibility!

I am not Christ nor am I pretending to be.

Quit judging me!

Too many people are making that claim when it is not the reality.

Let's get real about our identity:

It is my faith, not my dress,

Even if I look like a mess.

It is my faith, not my speech,

No, it isn't in the words I preach.

It is my faith, not my family life,

My life is overfilled with vice.

It is my faith, not how much money I give,

Even if I blow it by the way I live.

It is my faith, not how much Bible I know, even if I am living on death row.

It is my faith, not if I drink, even if the alcohol stinks.

It is my faith, not if I smoke, even if I smell of dope.

It is my faith, not if I am divorced,

Even if I chose that course.

It is my faith, not my worship attendance,

Even if in the church I am dependent.

It is my faith, not my moral life,

Even if I am sinful and unrepentant.

It is my faith, not my place, my race, my case, or my taste.

So, you have to meet me where I am in this race.

What you think about my life is not the basis of my faith,

It's on Jesus Christ, not you, that I rest my case.

I know it is my faith that has given me eternal life.

I am not tripping trying to live the Christian life.

IT'S FAITH, NOT INTELLECT

God came in the flesh in the person of Jesus Christ

And you better believe this if you want to do what is right.

It's not about good works or goodwill to all men,

None of those things will cleanse you from your sins.

Faith in Christ can save you from eternal damnation,

The lake of fire is the destiny of every unbelieving nation.

God came in the flesh in the person of Jesus Christ,

It's not philosophy or any manmade advice.

It's not logical, defies the scientific standards of life.

It's not accepted by the academic elite – the scholars and great thinkers of our time.

It's not accepted by the common laymen

Whose entangled lives leave them no time

to consider the incarnation of the divine.

The issue is faith and not intellect.

The very miracles that Christ performed defy logic.

Whether you were an eyewitness or you just came into the knowledge.

The task for you is still the same:

It is Faith and not what you learned in college.

Can Jehovah God – creator of Heaven and earth – put on flesh,

Become a man, die and come back to life again?

I learned this from my father and mother

Who drilled it into my head over and over again.

Until I believed through Jesus I am saved and born again.

Faith is something you will never understand,

It is something you must believe and you can.

It is only a matter of your intellect,

In that it was God's plan to give you a mind to understand

That Jesus Christ is God and Emmanuel as man.

It is not education,

It is not IQ,

It is not man's knowledge

Or anything in the realm of you.

It is the God within you,

He bears witness to your spirit that Jesus is true.

The one and only incarnation of God,

His bodily revelation was not a façade.

It is faith, not intellect

Because it transcends the material,

The natural, and the reasonable,

The things that people expect.

Faith is in a realm that is beyond what is feasible.

Our minds will except the reasonable and even the possible

But faith in Jesus as God for some is completely unbelievable.

It is faith. Not science

It is faith. Not reason

It is faith. Not tradition

It is faith. Not religion

It is faith. Make a decision!

SAVED OR HYPE?

*L*ord, when I got saved I thought everything would be all right.

Christ is in my life now, so my burdens are going to be light.

No more worries at night or if my husband's going to start acting right.

Maybe we'll catch up on our rent and not have to move out at night.

Lord, when I got saved I thought I wouldn't have any more fights,

No more violence on the streets or neighbors who don't act right

And I would like my new church family and they would treat me right.

Even my children would behave better and stay off the streets at night!

Lord, when I got saved you said my burdens would be light.

What happened to your promise? Or was it just all hype?

I look at my life and it's still imperfect!

For over a year I've been saved and my burdens still intersect.

I'm worried sick that I'm not going to have a place to stay tonight.

My husband's acting up, been in and out of jail all of his life.

As the trouble begins to rise in our life

We both go back to the same old vice.

Lord, am I saved or not? My God, what is my plight?

I am not making it in this Christian world;

It's easier to live in sin unfurled.

With everything going wrong and so full of strife

Why should I even try to live the Christian life?

Lord, when I got saved,

The preacher said just pray

And everything will be alright.

Now I know it was all just hype!

Why not just take mercy on me, and end my life?

MERCY, LORD, MERCY, ME

ercy, mercy, mercy,

Lord, have mercy on me!

For I was blind and couldn't see

The mercy and grace you have given to me.

How can I not be merciful to others I see,

When I'm depending on your mercy for me

And when I think about the mercy you have already shown to me.

I say, Father, forgive me for not having the same compassion you have shown me,

For walking on the street by the beggars who could have been me.

For not visiting the sick who want to see me

Or writing those in prison who want to hear from me

Or being there for loved ones who need me.

Lord, help me, to see the compassion that must be my reality

If it is Jesus I am truly trying to imitate, and see.

Lord, have mercy on me,

For I am a sinner trying to be

Your humble servant of grace and mercy.

GOD IS LOVE

∞

A LOVE SONG

*C*horus:

    God is love He's ev - ver - lasting

God is love He's long - suf –fering

God is love He's for – giv – ing

God is love His Love's a-mazing

God is love He's ev - ver - lasting

God is love He's long - suf –fering

God is love He's for – giv – ing

God is love His Love's a-mazing

1st Verse:

His Love is encompassing and abides in me and you

When He wakes me in the morning

His Love rains down like dew

It higher than the tallest mountain

And deeper than deepest sea

We can't escape the Love Jesus

Because He died for you and me.

Chorus:

God is love He's ev - ver - lasting

God is love He's long - suf –fering

God is love He's for – giv – ing

God is love His Love's a-mazing

God is love He's ev - ver - lasting

God is love He's long - suf –fering

God is love He's for – giv – ing

God is love His Love's a-mazing

2nd Verse

When I think about the love - of – God - And His sacrifice for Me.

I can't believe He died on -the –Cross - for a wretched soul like me.

I'm so grate-full to –have - life and to have it abundantly

I have given my life and soul – to - Christ from now to eternity.

Chorus:

God is love He's ev - ver - lasting

God is love He's long - suf –fering

God is love He's for – giv – ing

God is love His Love's a-mazing

God is love He's ev - ver - lasting

God is love He's long - suf –fering

God is love He's for – giv – ing

God is love His Love's a-mazing

Bridge:

Jesus is Lord - Savior of the World

Prophet and Priest -King of all Kings

The Lion of Judah, - the Ancient of Days

One day He'll come -and He will Reign

Chorus:

God is love He's ev - ver - lasting

God is love He's long - suf –fering

God is love He's for – giv – ing

God is love His Love's a-mazing

Bridge:

Jesus is Lord - Savior of the World

Prophet and Priest -King of all Kings

One day He'll come -and we will see

The faith that we have - is Reality

Chorus:

God is love He's ev - ver - lasting

God is love He's long - suf –fering

God is love He's for – giv – ing

God is love His Love's a-mazing

GRACE

*a*mazing is as the song says
Unreasonable in concept

Unthinkable in Reality

Wonderful in Acceptance

Powerful in Faith

Humbling in gratitude

Confidence in Salvation

Hopeful in expectation

Because I see now what I believe

That He Loves me, Amazingly Me

Of all people better than me

He Loves me. Just as I am

Without one plea, Just as He made Me

. . .

In flesh weak and dying every day

In Spirit longing and crying for the day

When I will be free

Of what is weak and decaying everyday

And live without limits in a world of no time

Just Love and Oneness with God Who is the Father of Time

I am grace personified

By the Christ who died

I am grace realized

By the Christ who is risen

And now lives in me.

Amazing Grace how sweet the sound

That saved a wretch like me.

I NEED MORE

I need more of everything
    I need more of what I don't even know I need more of
Just in case I have it already,
And whatever it is, I need more of it
I'm sure I do
at least I think I do
Or I feel I do.

More begs the question doesn't it?
Why does the word more even exist?
Can't we have enough?
Where did more come from?
Don't we have what we need?
If we don't know we have enough why not?

Maybe we don't know how...

To have enough

To be satisfied

To be fulfilled

To be happy

To be content

To be at peace

To be in a joyful state.

I just know I need more

There's a voice in my mind telling me I need more

Of whatever more is

That gives me a sense of satisfaction

A sense of fulfillment

Or the illusion of what I want to feel

Because what I have is not enough.

Or at least not enough

To make me ...happy? I don't know.

To make me fulfilled? I don't know.

To make me strong or stronger? I don't know.

To make me satisfied? I don't know.

To make me feel loved? I don't know.

. . .

I don't know if enough is even enough or,

When enough is enough.

But I know, instinctively know,

there is another person in me

listening and observing me.

Me, my mind and my thinking,

my body and my cravings for more.

I feel at times this observer of me

is communicating with me to be still,

as if I am the observer of me, the witness of me,

Telling me, not in words, but in silence

that I need nothing more than to know who I Am

and that the I Am in me is enough.

I am enough, because I Am is enough?

I don't need more?

I Am is communicating with and observing me.

Present with me and without form just like me.

I am flesh and bone, but also soul and spirit .

I and I Am are one and enough.

In the present and in silence where the

Souls and Spirits of man commune with the I Am.

I realize that I am more than I could ever imagine,

or contemplate in this life.

I am more than words can communicate,

or ideas can convey.

I am enough and I don't need more of

anything other than to be present.

I need nothing more.

THE ENEMY

The enemy,
known and unknown,

Seen and unseen,

Regardless of our state of consciousness,

He is present, he is real, he is involved,

he is active and he is committed

to our failures and the demise

of everything that is good and precious

in every aspect our lives.

The enemy

Finds joy in sadness, piece in chaos

He loves conflict, malice and violence

His specialty is brokenness and

Brokenness leads to despair

and despair leads to death.

The enemy

He has that kind of power you know,

The power of death but only in this life,

He has no power over eternal life

Eternal life was purchase with a price

far beyond what we could ever pay

It was that happy Day on Calvary

When Jesus Washed my sins away.

The enemy

His power is deceptive appearing weak

Making you feel stronger

When you are weaker than you think.

The Enemy

His Wisdom is seductive appealing to your intelligence

Feeding your ego and setting you up for hopelessness

Soon you realize His words are not life but

But death, Full emptiness and Lies.

The Enemy

Makes you think you are smarter than you actually are

Makes you believe that you can do wrong and get away with it.

Make you believe a lie and love it instead of truth.

Makes you celebrate evil and despise what is good.

Makes you seek wrong instead of right

Makes you embrace the darkness instead of the light

Makes you hate to love and love to fight.

The Enemy

He is all about strife

Making you feel larger than life

Tossing you here and there

When actually you are going nowhere

But to live a life of Hell.

Lord, by your sacrifice we quell

The Enemy.

DID YOU ENJOY THIS BOOK?

I sure hope so!

Please join our family and write a review. Reviews are the "tip jar" of the book publishing industry. New readers weigh reviews heavily in deciding to make a purchase. You being so generous as to share your experience is the lifeblood of the success of "The Power Poetry Collection".

I appreciate you!
Eric Lawrence Frazier

SCAN ME

THE POWER IS NOW MEDIA

The Power Is Now Media is an online multimedia company founded in 2009 by Eric L. Frazier MBA, headquartered in Riverside, California. We are advocates for homeownership, wealth building, and financial literacy. We create and publish original educational content about real estate through nationally syndicated Radio, Podcasts, Magazines, TV, Social Media, Streaming platforms, and special online seminars and webinars. We are an online platform and resource for everyone to learn about homeownership, housing, loan programs, and down payment assistance to achieve financial literacy and the American dream of homeownership. We are supported by housing finance agencies, real estate associations, and civic, religious, and community organizations. We help them amplify their voice about the services and programs they offer in lending, housing, and homeownership. Visit us at www.thepowerisnow.com

The Mission of the Power is Now Media is to inspire and educate consumers and real estate professionals to build wealth through the acquisition, management, and sale of real estate with information and support we provide via our website, live and on-demand TV, and social media platforms that empower everyone to own real estate now and achieve the American dream of homeownership. Our company slogan is "We are leading the conversation about real homeownership."

The Power Is Now Media corporate office is located at 3739 6th Street, Riverside, CA 92501. Telephone/Fax: 800-401-8994. Eric Lawrence Frazier MBA is a California Licensed Loan Originator (NMLS License #461807) and Real Estate Broker (License #O1148434).

ABOUT THE AUTHOR

Mr. Eric Lawrence Frazier MBA is the President, and CEO of The Power Is Now Media, The Power Is Now is a multimedia company that specializes in real estate education for consumers and real estate professionals on various topics in real estate, lending, economics, and government policy. The information is published on The Power Is Now Media website (www.thepowerisnow.com), national online radio and podcast platforms nationwide, Major social media channels, and live-stream TV platforms.

Mr. Frazier is also the publisher and editor-in-chief of The Power Is Now Magazines, which are online real estate magazines first published on September 1, 2013. These magazines focus on real estate education, real estate homes for sale, and national real estate news. Mr. Frazier is a graduate of Redlands University in Redlands, California, and has an MBA with an emphasis in finance and a BS in business administration and management. He has lectured at the University of California Riverside on the US mortgage crisis to international business leaders from India and has served as an adjunct professor.

With nearly four decades of originations, management, underwriting, operations, and marketing experience, Mr. Frazier is nationally known as a mortgage lending professional. He has over thirty years of experience in real estate sales as a licensed California real estate agent and over twenty years of experience as a real estate broker (#01143484).

He and his wife are the founders of Frazier Group Reality. (fraziergrouprealty.com), a-full-service,family-owned-and-operated real estate company in Riverside, California. Mr. Frazier is the former president of the Orange County Realtist, which was a chapter of the National Association of Real Estate Brokers (NAREB), and former director of the California Association of Real Estate Brokers. He is a former vice president of the Orange County National Association of Hispanic Real Estate Professionals and a former advisory board member of the Orange County Asian Real Estate Association of America.

He is also on the board of directors of the Riverside Fair Housing Council; the board of directors of Project Tomorrow (tomorrow.org), a national education nonprofit; a member of the 100 Black Men of America and the NAACP; a pastor; and leader of The Power Is Now Ministries. He is a member of the National Association of Mortgage Brokers, the Pacific West Realtors Association of Realtors, the California Association of Realtors (CAR), and the National Association of Realtors (NAR). He is the past president and director of the State of California African American Museum (www.caamuseum.org) and a former pastor of the North Fontana Church.

Mr. Frazier is also an author, singer, poet, and songwriter. He is a blogger, motivational speaker, business consultant, business coach for profit and non profit companies, and community leader. He enjoys golf, running, and jazz music. Mr. Frazier strives to be a role model for African American men and enjoys mentoring and coaching young people and adults. His greatest accomplishments are being married to the love of his life for over forty years and being the father of four daughters. His three oldest daughters have master's degrees in management and business, and his youngest daughter has a bachelor's degree in apparel merchandising and management. All of Mr. Frazier's accomplishments and associations can be found at www.linkedin.com/in/ericfrazier.

FOLLOW ME ON SOCIAL MEDIA

LET'S CONNECT ON LINKEDIN

www.ingramcontent.com/pod-product-compliance
Lightning Source LLC
Chambersburg PA
CBHW032141040426
42449CB00005B/353